Weather

The powerful forces and fragile resources of Earth

By Moira Butterfield

Ticktock

Contents

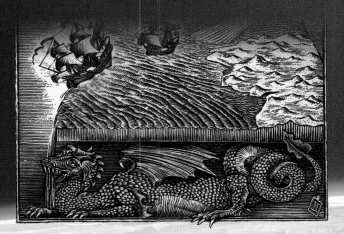

Weather

The powerful forces and fragile resources of Earth

An Hachette UK Company
www.hachette.co.uk

First published in Great Britain in 2015 by Ticktock,
an imprint of Octopus Publishing Group Ltd
Carmelite House
50 Victoria Embankment
London, EC4Y 0DZ
www.octopusbooks.co.uk
www.ticktockbooks.co.uk

ISBN 978 1 78325 238 1

A CIP record for this book is available from the British Library.

Printed and bound in China
1 3 5 7 9 10 8 6 4 2

Design: Dan and Amanda Newman/Perfect Bound Ltd
Diagrams: Collaborate Agency
Creative Director: Miranda Snow
Commissioning Editor: Anna Bowles
Managing Editor: Karen Rigden
Production controller: Meskerem Berhane

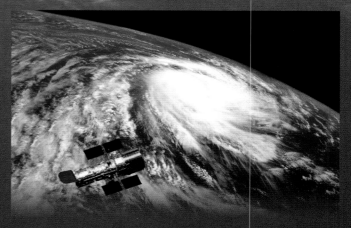

Chapter 1: Gods and explorers
Magic weather

Long ago, people thought that gods and goddesses controlled the weather and stirred up storms if they were in a bad temper!

I'm Snowy and this is my friend Sunny. We're going to be your wonderful world weather guides.

Let's start with some sky stories from long ago!

Apollo, the Greek god of light

The Ancient Greeks believed that gods and goddesses controlled the weather from their home on the top of a mountain. Different Greek gods had different weather powers. For instance, **Apollo**, the god of light, drove the Sun across the sky every day in his chariot. Meanwhile **Aeolus** (left) ruled the winds and kept them locked inside a floating island.

The Ancient Romans were sure that gods interfered with the weather when they were angry. **Neptune**, the Roman god of the sea (left), whipped up storms and Jupiter, the leader of the gods, hurled lightning bolts. Roman priests made sacrifices at temples to persuade them not to have weather tantrums.

In the ancient Mayan city of Chichen Itza, in Mexico, there is a 1,000-year-old temple called El Castillo. It was once dedicated to a god called **Kukulcan**, a giant feathery serpent (right) who was said to move the winds with his tail.

Ancient weather gods were often pictured as magical animals. For instance, North American tribes believed in a giant eagle god called the **Thunderbird** who flapped his wings to create thunder and shot lightning from his eyes. The thunderbird would sometimes appear at the top of their totem poles (left).

Discovering weather

In the late 1400s and the 1500s, European sailors began to discover new lands. They had very little equipment to predict the weather, so they had to rely on their knowledge of clouds, winds and waves to help them navigate safely.

When the first European explorers returned from their voyages, they passed information on to **map-makers**, who began to draw the first accurate maps. The map-makers marked the weather on their charts, too. They sometimes drew the winds as faces with puffed-out cheeks as though blowing air.

Although they couldn't predict the weather, sailors feared certain parts of the sea which they knew were **stormy**. They gave these locations weather-based names. For instance, the southern tip of Africa was named *The Cape of Storms*. Then the King of Portugal, realizing the name was scaring sailors and being keen to keep his fleet of merchant ships at sea, renamed it *The Cape of Good Hope*.

The **first** measure

Gradually, people began to realize that weather was related to changes in **air pressure** (its weight). In 1643, Italian Evangelista Torricelli made the first **barometer** to measure air pressure:

1 Torricelli filled a long glass tube with mercury and placed it upside-down in a bowl of mercury.

2 The mercury rose up in the tube if air pressure was high, and pushed down on the mercury in the bowl.

3 The mercury sank down in the tube if air pressure lowered and did not press down so strongly on the mercury in the bowl.

Torricelli's invention was the beginning of scientific weather prediction. You can find out more about the effect air pressure has on weather on p14.

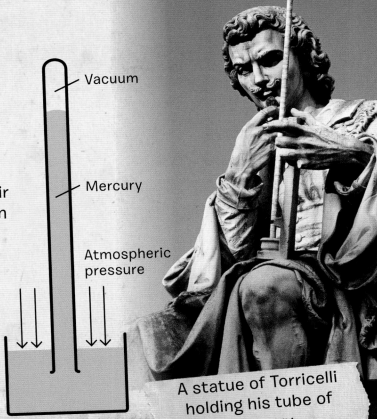

Vacuum

Mercury

Atmospheric pressure

A statue of Torricelli holding his tube of mercury

Moon warnings

Before weather-predicting equipment was invented, sailors had to look out day and night for weather signs in the sky. They knew that if they saw a halo around the moon, a storm was probably on its way.

Phew! It's lucky penguins don't go on boat trips!

Chapter 2: What is weather anyway?

What does 'weather' mean?

Weather is the name we use to describe the state things such as temperature, sunshine, wind and rainfall within the Earth's atmosphere. Weather is constantly happening and changes in the weather are related to the tiny air molecules that are around us.

The Earth is surrounded by a layer of air called the **atmosphere.** Weather is the name we give to changes in the atmosphere which lead to clouds, wind and rain. Most of the **air molecules** in the atmosphere are in the region closest to the Earth's surface, called the **troposphere.** This stretches to roughly 14 km (8.6 miles) above sea level, and it's here that weather occurs.

A satellite above a hurricane

Weather is what happens in the air every day, and **climate** is the average measurement of weather conditions over a long time, usually 30 years

Weather = *It's snowing today.*

Climate = *It's cold here every winter.*

The Sun's heat is absorbed by our planet's surface. This heat then slowly radiates (is released) from the surface and heats the air above. Changes in the amount of heat radiated from the Earth lead to the air molecules either warming or cooling, which makes them move in different ways (see p15). This movement helps to create weather.

Don't bother inventing an umbrella for astronauts!

Space weather is even wilder!

Earth's Atmosphere

The atmosphere has five layers. Weather occurs in the bottom-most layer, nearest the Earth.

The exosphere (500-8,000 km/ 300-5,000 miles high). The highest level, where weather satellites orbit. The temperature is very hot. There are hardly any air molecules.

The thermosphere (80-500 km/50-300 miles high). The International Space Station orbits here.

The mesosphere (50-80 km/ 30-50 miles high). The higher you go in the mesosphere, the colder the temperature.

The stratosphere (18-50 km/10-30 miles high). Aircraft fly up here to avoid weather below.

The troposphere (the bottom level, from sea level to around 14 km (8.7 miles high). Contains lots of air molecules and water vapour (water molecules floating in the air). Weather happens here.

Seasons and climate

The Earth isn't standing still. It spins round once every 24 hours, giving us day and night, and it is also moving round the Sun. That's why we have **seasons** and there are different **climates** all over the world.

The Earth is round, but because it has a tilt on its axis, the sun's rays do not fall evenly across our planet's surface. The rays shine directly on to the Earth's **Equator** (the imaginary line around its middle) but they are more spread out towards the North Pole, at the top of the Earth, and the South Pole, at the bottom. That's why areas around the Equator have a generally warm temperature, whereas areas towards the poles are cooler.

This amount of sun energy is spread over more of the Earth near the poles.

The same amount of sun energy covers a much smaller part of the Earth at the Equator.

So the Equator gets hotter than the poles.

Midnight sun
Because the North and South Poles are at an angle to the Sun, they each get six months of continuous daylight and six months of continuous chilly darkness.

Climate zones are created by the way the Sun's rays fall on different parts of the Earth. There are six main climate zones which all have different seasonal weather:

Polar - very cold and dry all year
Temperate - cold winters and mild summers
Arid - dry, hot all year
Tropical - hot and wet all year
Mediterranean - mild winters, dry hot summers
Mountains (tundra) - very cold all year

The Earth moves around the Sun in an elliptical (oval-shaped) orbit. It takes 365 ¼ days to go round once, and it isn't vertical in space as it travels. It's tilted slightly. For a few months each year half of the Earth is tilted towards the Sun and gets strong heat rays, while the other half is tilted away and gets weak rays. The position gradually reverses through the year, giving us our seasons.

Spring in the Northern Hemisphere, Autumn in the Southern Hemisphere

Winter in the Northern Hemisphere, Summer in Southern Hemisphere

Summer in the Northern Hemisphere, Winter in the Southern Hemisphere

Autumn in the Northern Hemisphere, Spring in the Southern Hemisphere

All about air

The way that air behaves creates the world's weather. So what do those tiny **air molecules** do exactly?

The weight of air, called **air pressure**, gets heavier the closer it is to the Earth's surface. You could imagine it by thinking of a human pyramid. The people at the bottom have to bear the weight of all the people above, so they have the most pressure on them. That's true of the air at sea level too.

So **that's** what air does!

In the 1600s French scientist Blaise Pascal discovered that air pressure varied according to height. He measured the air pressure on the ground and sent a friend up a mountain to measure the air pressure up there. Then he compared the two results.

Air: 3 top facts

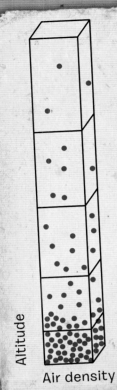

Altitude

Air density

1 The greater the air pressure, the more molecules of air there are, all squashed up closely together. The number of air molecules is called the air density.

2 50% of all the Earth's air is in the bottom 5 km (3.1 miles) of atmosphere, where it is most dense. No wonder there's so much weather down there!

3 The higher up in the atmosphere, the fewer air molecules there are and the wider apart they are. And as there are fewer air molecules there will also be fewer oxygen molecules – so that's mountain climbers need to take oxygen with them.

Active air

Here's what happens when air molecules change temperature:

Going up – When air is warmed it rises. The air molecules move faster and bump into each other, spreading apart. The pressure falls as the air becomes less dense. You can see the effect of air rising if you watch a hot air balloon. The air inside the balloon is heated up by the balloon's flame, and it starts to rise, taking the balloon with it.

Going down – When air is cooled it sinks downwards. The air molecules move more slowly and become closer together. The pressure rises.

The big circle – There's a constant cycle of air warming, rising, cooling and falling in the Earth's atmosphere. It may look empty but it's a busy place!

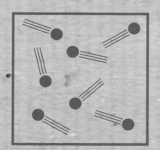

Air molecules in warm air

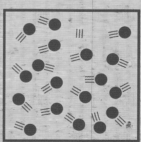

Air molecules in cool air

All this moving air is making me dizzy!

Getting warm

The air is warmed by the sun's **heat** radiating from the Earth, but that heat is not always the same. The variations help to create weather changes.

2 All over the world there are different surfaces – such as land, ocean, rock or forest – radiating heat differently and heating up the air at different rates.

Dark tarmac reflects more heat than pale earth

Big cities radiate lots of heat from concrete buildings

1 Different **surfaces radiate heat** in different ways. You can feel this on a hot day. Touch a rock and you'll feel that it's warm or even hot. It's radiating lots of heat fast. Touch some soil and you'll find it feels cooler. It's radiating heat more slowly. Because of this the air molecules above the soil will heat up more slowly than the ones above the rock.

Who knew that air was so lively!

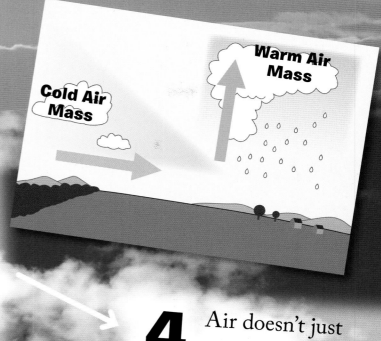

Cold Air Mass

Warm Air Mass

3 Warm air weighs less than cold air. **Warm air rises**, and **cold air sinks**. When warm air rises, cold air flows in underneath it. You can feel this happening because it's this air movement that causes wind (see p22).

4 Air doesn't just warm up and rise at a different rate over one patch of concrete or soil. It rises at different rates around the whole planet – over oceans, deserts, plains, ice sheets and jungles. There's an awful lot of air moving around all the time!

5 Because air molecules are warmed and cooled at different rates in different places, there are areas of warm air or cold air moving around the world. They are called **air masses**. Imagine them as giant bubbles of air that have different temperatures and pressures.

It's possible to see air masses causing weather changes by taking pictures in space

Pressure patterns

Air pressure is shown by lines on a weather map - which you might see on TV. These lines are called isobars.

You'll see these **isobars** lines on weather maps. They look like the height contours you'll see on ordinary maps, but they link up locations where the air pressure is the same. Air generally moves along the isobars - and from the isobars we can roughly predict the **wind direction** and speed.

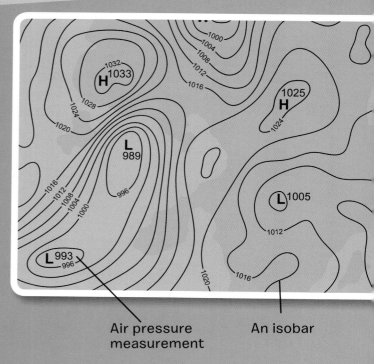

Air pressure measurement

An isobar

Those weather guys are under a lot of pressure!

Isobars: 3 top facts

1 Air pressure is measured in **millibars** or kiloPascals. Under 1,000 millibars (100 kiloPascals) is low pressure.

2 High pressure is between 1,025 and 1,050 millibars (102.5–105 kiloPascals).

3 If the isobars on a map are close together then the pressure will change a lot over a short distance. This helps to create strong winds.

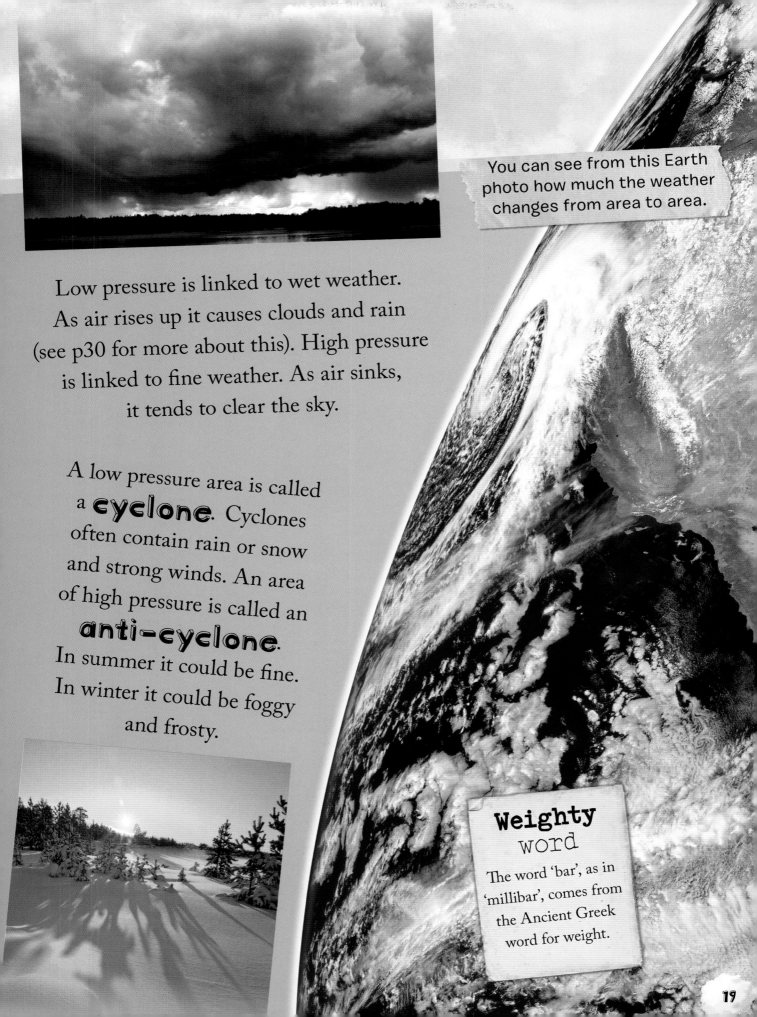

You can see from this Earth photo how much the weather changes from area to area.

Low pressure is linked to wet weather. As air rises up it causes clouds and rain (see p30 for more about this). High pressure is linked to fine weather. As air sinks, it tends to clear the sky.

A low pressure area is called a **cyclone**. Cyclones often contain rain or snow and strong winds. An area of high pressure is called an **anti-cyclone**. In summer it could be fine. In winter it could be foggy and frosty.

Weighty word

The word 'bar', as in 'millibar', comes from the Ancient Greek word for weight.

Here come the fronts

You might hear TV weather presenters talk about **weather fronts**, which are marked on their maps. When a weather front turns up you can expect some changes in the weather!

A weather front can look like a line of clouds moving into blue sky.

A weather **front** is the place where two big **air masses** meet. The air in each air mass could be behaving very differently from each other. One front might be cold while another is warm, and when different fronts meet it usually means a **weather change**.

Fronts were discovered by Norwegian **Vilhelm Bjerknes** who named them after armies meeting at a battlefront.

Putting up a front

When a cold air mass pushes into a warm air mass, the area between the two is called a cold front. It is marked on a weather map with a line of triangles. The tips of the triangles point in the direction the cold air is moving. The cold air moves underneath the warm air because it is denser. The warm air rises quickly, often leading to rain. Find out why on p30.

When a warm air mass moves towards a cold air mass the area between the two is called a warm front. It is marked on a weather map as a line of semi-circles. The semi-circles point in the direction the warm air is moving. The warm air rises up over the cold air, and again it usually brings rain.

Cold front

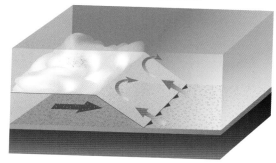

Warm front

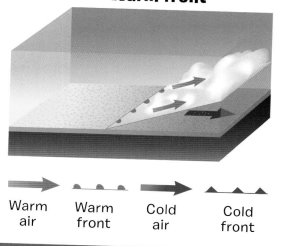

Warm air   Warm front   Cold air   Cold front

If you hear a weather forecaster talking about an **active or weak front**, they are describing the difference in temperature between the air masses that are meeting up. If a very cold air mass meets a very warm air mass, then the front is usually an active one and there is likely to be a big weather change. If there isn't much difference between the two air masses, the front is a weak one and there won't be such a big change in the weather.

Chapter 3: Hold onto your hat!

Speedy wind

Wind is created when air moves quickly. Air can gently swoosh along in a breeze, blow fairly intensely or tear through the sky.

One of the **fastest wind** speeds ever recorded was during a tropical storm on 10th April, 1996 on Barrow Island, off the coast of Western Australia when a gust reached 408 kph (253 mph). The winds inside the spiraling funnel of air in a tornado are likely to move much faster (see p68), but it's very difficult to measure them accurately.

The Beaufort Scale

In 1805 British Navy Admiral Sir Francis Beaufort devised a scale of 12 numbers to describe wind strength and how wind affects land and sea. It is called the **Beaufort Scale**, and is still used today. Here are some examples.

0 – Calm. Smoke rises straight up from bonfires and chimneys. The sea is flat.

3 – A gentle breeze. Leaves rustle in the trees. There are small wavelets on the sea.

6 – A strong breeze. Umbrellas turn inside out. There are foaming crests on waves.

12 – A hurricane. There could be damage to trees and buildings. Out on the ocean there are huge waves.

We can measure the **speed of wind** using an **anemometer**. It has three or four cups mounted on arms. When the wind catches the cups the arms spin round, and a dial counts the number of spins. The higher the number of spins the faster the wind.

A tornado over Rozel, Kansas, USA

Eroded rocks at Gold Butte, Nevada, USA

Over time, the wind can change even the shape of rocks! This kind of **erosion** (wearing down of the landscape) is called the **aeolian process**, after the Ancient Greek wind god Aeolus. The weird rocks shown here were created by the wind picking up sand particles and smashing them against the rock, gradually wearing down the surface.

Wind really blows

Which way the wind?

We can work out the direction of the wind by using a compass. The way the wind blows has a big effect on the weather.

We use compass points to describe **wind direction**. So you might hear someone saying that a wind is 'north-easterly' or 'south-easterly', for instance. They're not telling you where the wind is blowing *to*. They're telling you where the wind is blowing *from*.

If a wind is coming from the sea, it is likely to be carrying lots of water vapour that it has picked up from the ocean. It might well bring fog or rain with it. If the wind is coming from the land it is likely to be drier.

Sea and land breezes

The seaside is often a windy spot! That's because of the differences between land and sea. Land radiates the Sun's heat more quickly than water. The land cools more quickly, too. Here's what happens:

Daytime – During the day the air over the land warms, expands and rises, and cooler, denser air rushes in from above the sea. This is called a sea breeze.

Nighttime – At night, the land cools quickly. Now the air above the ocean is warmer and rising, so the cooler, denser air rushes in from above the land. This is called a land breeze.

Daytime: sea breeze

Nighttime: land breeze

Veering and Backing

Winds can easily change direction. If a wind changes direction clockwise – from south to west, for instance – it is called a *veering* wind. If it changes direction anticlockwise – from south to east, for instance – it is called a *backing* wind.

A **prevailing wind** means a wind that generally blows one way over a location. You can sometimes see trees sloping over where they have grown away from a prevailing wind that has blown over them for most of their lives.

All around the world

Because of the differences in temperature between air above the Equator and air above the poles, and the spin of the Earth, there are some **world winds** that reliably blow in the lower half of the troposphere.

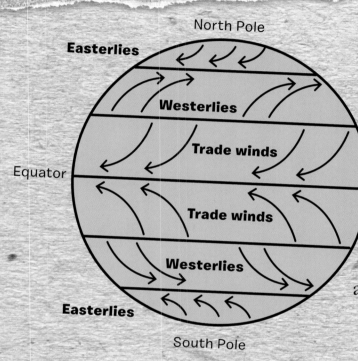

North Pole

Easterlies

Westerlies

Trade winds

Equator

Trade winds

Westerlies

Easterlies

South Pole

The regular system of world winds includes the **Westerlies**, the **Easterlies** and the **trade winds**. Because their direction is so constant, sailors use them to help plan their voyages. These winds have a big effect on our weather, too, moving water vapour around and changing air temperature.

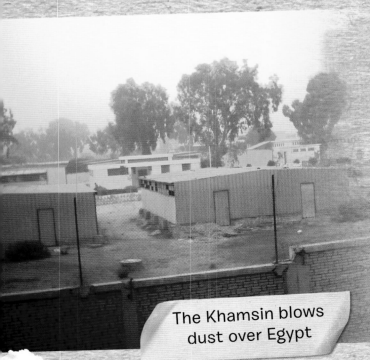

The Khamsin blows dust over Egypt

Local winds

People in some areas can rely on local winds blowing at certain times of the year. These winds are often given specific names. Here are two famous examples:

Mistral – A fierce cold wind that tears across southern France towards the sea in winter and springtime. If it blows for a long time it is said to drive people mad!

Khamsin – A hot dry dusty wind that blows across North Africa in early spring. Its name means '50' because it can blow for 50 days.

Clouds mark a jet stream, a river of high wind seen from space.

Jet streams are fast-flowing **rivers of air** between 9-26 km (5–16 miles) high above Earth. Nobody knew they existed until aeroplanes began to fly at high altitudes (heights) in the 1940s. Jet streams form between the cold air above the poles and the warmer air further from the poles.

Faster flights

Passenger aeroplanes sometimes fly along jet streams, using the power of the wind to help them go faster.

It's a windy world!

The **Doldrums** are regions of the Atlantic and Pacific Oceans, near the Equator, where the sea is often calm with no wind. The calm is caused by air conditions that occur when two trade winds meet. Sailors have always dreaded crossing the Doldrums because the weather is **unpredictable**. A sailing ship could get stuck there for weeks in the windless heat or, without warning, face violent storms.

Whirling energy

Sometimes you might see **wind turbines** scattered across the landscape. When they are turning they are creating power from the wind.

A **wind farm** is a group of wind turbines all in the same spot. They might be on a windy hill or even on platforms out at sea. The world's biggest wind farm is the Gansu Wind Farm project in China. It already has over 5,000 giant turbines, and won't be complete until 2020, when many more turbines will stretch across this windy desert region.

Not all turbines look like windmills. Look out for wind spires, which have long tall propellers that extend vertically instead of spinning around horizontally. Wind spires are good for places where there isn't much space, such as in cities.

The largest vertical wind turbine, in Canada, is 110 m (360 ft) tall

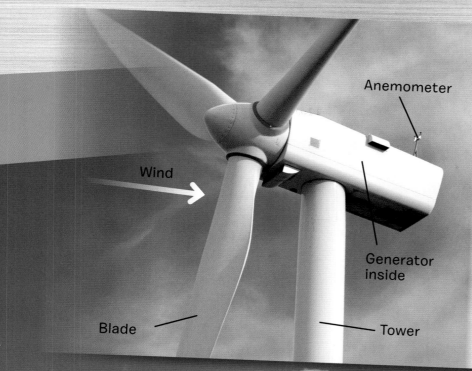

Anemometer

Wind →

Generator inside

Blade

Tower

How it works

A wind turbine has two or three propeller blades attached to a shaft. When the blades are caught by the wind they spin the shaft, which in turn spins a generator to create electricity. If the wind gets too strong (usually around 88 kph/55 mph) the wind turbine will automatically turn off to stop the blades getting damaged.

Wind turbines can send electricity to a national grid for everyone to use, or just provide power for one building. For instance, the Bahrain World Trade Centre (left) has its own wind turbines to create its electricity. They are built between two halves of the skyscraper. The building halves are shaped like sails to funnel the wind across the turbines in the middle.

A wind farm near Cadiz in Spain

Our invisible water world

What do people and fish have in common? They're both surrounded by water! But don't panic. You don't need to start swimming, because the water around *you* is invisible. It's floating in the air as **water vapour.**

Warm air can hold more water vapour than cold air. When air cools to a certain point (called its **dew point**), the water vapour **condenses**, which means it turns into **tiny droplets**. Suddenly it is visible. You can see this for yourself on a cold day - as you exhale your warm breath turns cold, the water vapour condenses and mist appears.

How wet?

The amount of water vapour that air can carry is called its relative **humidity**. When air has as much water vapour as it can possibly carry, we say it has 100% relative humidity.

Thank goodness we're waterproof!

The water cycle

How does water vapour get into the air?

Going up – 71% of the Earth's surface is covered in oceans, rivers and lakes. The Sun heats up this water every day, turning some of it into water vapour. This is called **evaporation**. Millions of litres of water evaporate in this way every day across the world.

Turning into droplets – Once it has evaporated, the water vapour floats upwards in rising air. As the rising air cools, the water vapour condenses into droplets, creating clouds.

Coming down – The droplets bump into each other and gradually get bigger, eventually falling as rain.

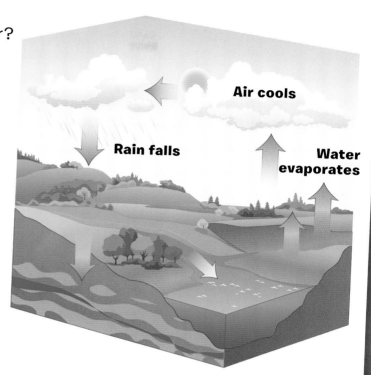

Air cools

Rain falls

Water evaporates

The whole process is called the water cycle because water is leaving and returning to the planet continually, circulating round and round.

The **water cycle** is vital to life on our planet. Plants suck it up through their roots and animals drink it. We even need water to create electricity – it turns the turbines in hydro-electricity power stations. Next time you feel fed up because it's cloudy and wet, remember... we need that rain to fall!

Clouds captured here!

High in the air water droplets gather around tiny dust or salt specks floating in the atmosphere. They begin to gather together, forming clouds.

Wet and **weeny**

Water droplets in a cloud are on average around 10-15 microns wide. A human hair is around 40 microns wide (a micron is 0.0001 mm/0.00004 in)

A good place to see a cloud is on top of a high mountain. When air meets the mountain it is forced to rise upwards. The rising air cools as it gets higher and water vapour condenses. Some mountains have a permanent cloud on top, like a fluffy white hat!

Today I saw a cloud shaped like an elephant.

Wow! You'll need to get a bigger umbrella!

Cloud families

The shape of a cloud is complicated! It depends on how high the base or bottom of the cloud is, its temperature and the way the air is behaving around it. We put clouds into groups, depending on their height and shape, and we give the groups Latin name-beginnings. Here are some name beginnings to listen out for:

Cirro- High clouds (base around 6,000 m/ 19,685 ft high) start with the word 'cirro', which means 'wisp of hair' in Latin.

Alto- Medium clouds (base around 2,000 m –6,000 m/ 6,561–19,685 ft high) start with the word 'alto', which means 'high' in Latin.

Strato- Clouds that look like a wide, unbroken sheet of cloud start with the word 'strato', which means 'layer'.

Cumulo- Clouds that billow upwards start with the name 'cumulo' which means 'heaped'.

Nimbo- Clouds that start with 'nimbo', meaning 'rain', are likely to provide us with rain or snow.

You'll sometimes see a long line of cloud, called a **contrail**, or vapour trails, behind a jet plane high in the sky. It's created when hot air loaded with water vapour shoots out of the jet engine and cools down. The water vapour condenses to make the contrail.

Cloud-spotting: Zone 1

Take a look at these common clouds captured on camera. Next time you see them you'll be able to name them and amaze your friends with your weather genius!

Cumulus
Fluffy clouds you'll see in fine weather. They are created when sunshine warms up a small parcel of moist air that rises up quickly and cools.

Stratus
A low-level foggy layer of cloud that might bring rain or snow.

Stratocumulus
Low-level lumpy cloud. Its name means 'flattened heap' and could signal light rain.

Cirrus
High wisps of cloud. They signal that the weather is likely to change.

I can tell that rain is coming by looking at the sky.

Altostratus
A grey layer covering the whole sky. A sign of heavy rain to come.

Altocumulus
Grey puffy clouds that come with changing weather fronts.

Nimbostratus
Dark low grey clouds full of rain or snow.

Cirrostratus
A thin high cloud sheet, so thin you can see the Sun or Moon through it. It can mean that rain or snow is on the way.

So can I. I just got a raindrop in my eye!

Cloud-spotting: Zone 2

These clouds either signal severe weather or they are quite rare. If you spot one of the unusual ones you can count yourself a lucky weather expert!

Lenticular

A very unusual cloud that looks like a flying saucer. It is formed by a particular pattern of winds blowing over mountains.

Cirrocumulus

Long rows of small clouds that look like the skin of a fish (some people call them a mackerel sky, after the markings on a mackerel fish). They are usually linked with approaching warm weather fronts, but in tropical regions they can signal a hurricane (see p64).

I like the sound of fishy clouds!

Supersonic
sky

When an aeroplane goes supersonic (faster than the speed of sound) it creates an area of low air pressure behind it. The air behind the plane suddenly cools and creates an unusual-looking round cloud behind the aircraft.

Cumulonimbus
A toweringly-high cloud with its top flattened out in the shape of an anvil (a wedge). The top of the anvil is flattened by strong winds, bringing thunderstorms with them.

Cloud iridescence
When clouds seem to have their own beautiful rainbow colours. This is caused when the Sun bounces off water droplets or ice crystals in the cloud.

37

Down comes the rain

Once water droplets form they can start to bump into each other, getting bigger and bigger until they are so heavy they fall as rain.

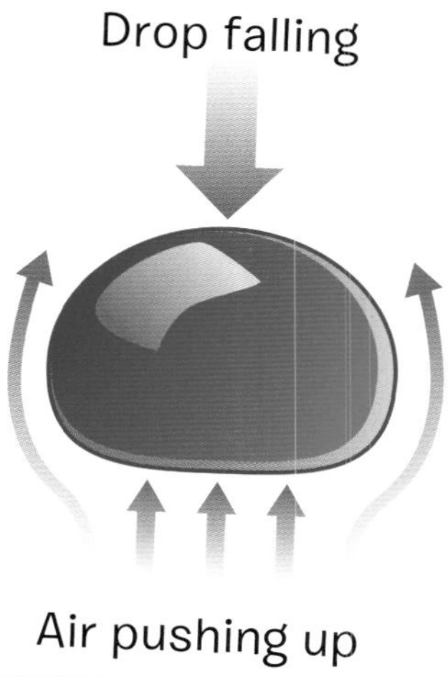

Drop falling

Air pushing up

Raindrops are usually drawn shaped like teardrops, but really they look more like the top half of a burger bun. As it falls, a raindrop gets flattened on the bottom but is curved on top like a dome.

You might see a **rainbow** when the sun is low in the sky behind you and it's raining. As light from the sun travels through the raindrops in front of you, it is **refracted** (bent). Light is made up of seven colours, and each colour is bent at a different angle as it comes out of the drops. The result is seven different curves of colour, side-by-side in the sky.

Recording **rain**

Meteorologists can work out how much rain falls in a place by putting a rain gauge outside, marked with measurements. Each time it rains the gauge fills and the level is recorded so that the average rainfall can be measured over time.

Rockets being fired from a plane to seed clouds

Cloud-seeding is a way of **making rain** happen by adding more particles to clouds, to encourage raindrops to form. Cloud-seeding was used in Beijing, China, before the opening ceremony of the 2008 Olympics. More than 1,000 rockets full of tiny chemical crystal particles were fired up into clouds to make it rain and clear the sky before the ceremony began.

Super **rain stats**

▶ Around 16 million tonnes of raindrops fall to Earth every second.

▶ The average speed of a raindrop is 8 kph (5 mph), though they have been known to speed down at 35 kph (22 mph). That would really sting if it hit you!

I don't like rain when it bounces off my beak!

Which rain today?

Rain can be drizzly or pelting and it can even be destructive. Over many years its power can change the shape of the landscape.

The result of heavy rain in Kenya

Rain can **wash away** soil, gradually changing the landscape over time. Just one heavy rainstorm is capable of washing away 1 mm (0.3 inches) of bare soil, and though that doesn't sound much, it can build up over time. Plants can help to prevent soil from being washed away.

Rain can gradually wear down soft rock such as sandstone. One famous example is the Bungle Bungle Range in Western Australia. The funny-looking sandstone towers there were once mountains, but they have been **worn down** by rain and wind over millions of years. Erosion by rain is called **weathering.**

Types of rain

A raindrop over 0.55mm wide is officially called rain. A raindrop less than 0.5mm wide is officially called drizzle. Drizzle doesn't make a splash when it falls in a puddle. When both rain and snow fall together it's called sleet. This happens when snow warms up as it falls and some of it turns to rain.

Cracking **rock**

Sometimes rain seeps into rock cracks, then freezes when it gets cold at night. When water freezes it expands, making the crack bigger. If this happens again and again, the rock will eventually shatter.

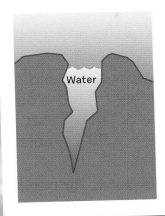

Water

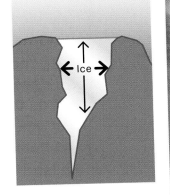

Ice

Damaged trees in Virginia, USA

Acid rain is caused by **pollution**, and it is so acidic that over time it can eat into stonework, kill plants and pollute rivers. It's caused when lots of waste gases from factories, power stations and car exhausts react with the water and oxygen in the air to create acid chemicals which dissolve into raindrops.

Big rains

In some parts of the world, heavy rain always sweeps in at certain times of the year, after a long dry spell. These are called monsoon rains, named after the winds that bring them.

Winds of change

Monsoon winds blow for six months one way and then six months the other way.

- In the summer, the air above the land heats up and rises, and air from the ocean flows in towards the land. The air that comes in over the ocean is full of moisture which falls as heavy rain.

- In winter the land cools down. Air begins to move the other way – from the land towards the ocean, creating a period of very dry weather.

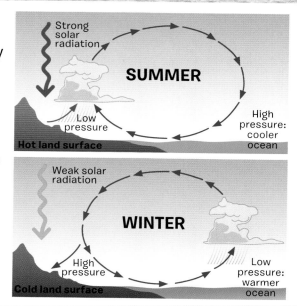

SUMMER

Strong solar radiation

Low pressure

Hot land surface

High pressure: cooler ocean

WINTER

Weak solar radiation

High pressure

Cold land surface

Low pressure: warmer ocean

Monsoons can cause floods such as this scene in Thailand in 2011.

Each year regions across southern Asia and parts of central Africa have heavy monsoon rains for months, beginning around springtime. Some 40% of the world's population lives in this 'monsoon belt', and the rains are usually welcome because they bring drinking water and water for crops.

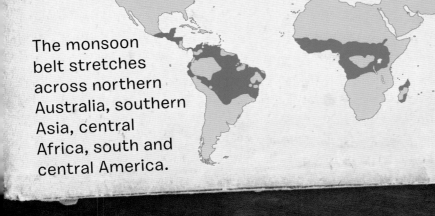

The monsoon belt stretches across northern Australia, southern Asia, central Africa, south and central America.

A herd of wildebeest cross the Serengeti Plain in Tanzania

In Africa the monsoon rains cause the world's largest **animal migration**. Around March every year, when the rains end and the grass on Serengeti Plain in Tanzania starts to dry up, more than two million wildebeest, zebra and other creatures leave and follow the movement of the rains to the Masai Mara in Kenya, where there is plenty of grass to eat. They will journey back the other way in October time when the rain returns.

Picking tea in the Assam hills during monsoon season

Cherrapunji is in the hills of Assam in northern India. It is one of the **world's wettest** locations during monsoon time between March and November. In 1995 a world rain record was set here when 2,493 mm (98 in) of rain fell in just 48 hours.

Fearsome floods

Heavy rain can bring dangerous flooding when rivers burst their banks.

A **flood plain** is an area of low-lying land alongside a river, and it is likely to be flooded if heavy rain swells the river. A whopping 80% of Bangladesh, in southern Asia, is on a huge flood plain around three giant rivers – the Ganges, the Brahmaputra and the Meghna. In 1998, unusually heavy monsoon rain caused the rivers to burst their banks causing unstoppable floods that affected over 30 million people.

Dhakka, the capital of Bangladesh, is on a river and often suffers from monsoon flooding.

Mudslides are caused when heavy rain dislodges soil and rock from hillsides. The mixture of water, soil and stones slides down like a liquid avalanche, engulfing everything in its path. Mudslides can travel very fast – up to 129 kph (80mph)!

If there is a sudden downpour the ground can quickly become saturated, (unable to soak up any more water). Instead the water flows over the surface of the ground and into gullies, drains and rivers. If a river is in a steep and narrow valley the sudden rain can make it flood very quickly. This is called **flash flooding** and because it can happen very quickly it can be very **dangerous**.

Protecting a city

Flood barriers are built to prevent rivers flooding. One of the largest in the world is the Thames Barrier (right) in London, UK. Ten giant steel gates span the river and can be closed to prevent storm surges – for example when very heavy rain flows out of the river and but is then pushed back by the tide.

Sound the fog horn!

Did you know that if you are walking through fog, you are actually walking through a cloud? **Fog** is a type of cloud that forms at ground level.

Fog forms when air full of moisture cools near the ground. The water in the air condenses into tiny **floating droplets**. The larger and closer together the droplets are, the thicker the fog.

Mist is formed in the same way as fog. It's just thinner, with smaller droplets.

Either it's foggy or my feathers are in my eyes!

The little Namib desert beetle is a champion fog-user. It lives on the southwest coast of Africa in one of the world's driest deserts, where the only moisture available is fog that rolls in from the sea. The beetle's hardened forewings are covered in tiny bumps that gather water and channel it down to the beetle's mouth.

Some locations get regular fog, especially places near the coast where the air tends to be full of water vapour. **San Francisco**, USA, is known as 'Fog City' because it is famous for its summer fog, which forms when warm, moist summer air meets cool ocean waters in San Francisco Bay.

Some communities **harvest** or 'collect' fog to use as drinking water. The villagers of Cabazane, in a very dry but foggy area of South Africa, get their water supply this way. Fog condenses on nylon mesh fog nets strung between poles, and the water drips down into guttering to be collected.

Smog alert

When fog combines with pollution it can turn into a dangerous dirty haze called smog.

When fog mixes with particles of smoke it turns to **smog**, a **yellowish mist** that can bring on a choking feeling if you breathe it in. In the past, when coal-burning was the only way to heat homes and run factories, cities were occasionally shrouded in this type of smog.

A coal-burning power station in Thailand

In certain weather conditions, when air stays in one place and there is plenty of sunlight, pollution particles such as nitrogen oxide and unburned engine fuel can create a poisonous type of haze called **photochemical smog**. The particles react to strong sunlight, producing a toxic mix of chemicals. Big cities with lots of traffic and industry tend to suffer from this type of smog.

Poo! Smog is stinky as well as sooty!

The world's most industrialized polluted areas are its smoggiest spots. Linfen in China is said to be the smoggiest city on the planet. Its **factory pollution** produces smog so thick that it can be hard to see anything through the browny-yellow air (right).

Seeing Black

In a busy city you may find tiny black specks on your windowsill. These are particles of soot from vehicle exhausts, and they help to form smog.

In cities where smog is common some people wear anti-pollution masks

Smog alerts are sometimes given out when the weather and pollution combine to create danger to human health. When smog levels are high, young children and people with illnesses are advised to stay inside.

Chapter 5: The big chill
The white stuff

When the temperature is very cold, the water vapour in the air starts to freeze into **ice crystals** instead of raindrops. Soon it's time to start making snowmen!

When the air temperature drops below 2°C (35.6°F), water vapour gathers around dust particles in the air and freezes to make tiny ice crystals. The ice crystals join up to make **snowflakes** that become heavy enough to fall out of the sky.

Ice crystals are tiny, but if you looked at a snowflake through a microscope you would see the crystals joined together in a six-sided (hexagonal) shape. All snowflakes are hexagonal, but apart from that they all look different. That's because of the unique conditions in the air when they formed.

Snowflakes that fall through dry, cool air are small and dry. They make powdery snow. When the temperature in the air is warmer, snowflakes melt around the edges and stick together, becoming bigger, damper flakes. This snow is the best for making **snowmen** and snowballs because it sticks together.

Faking **it**

Ski resorts need snow so they can stay in business! If it doesn't fall naturally, snow cannons can be used to make artificial snow. Water and pressurized air are forced through a snow cannon along with tiny particles of protein. The compressed air splits the water into droplets and cools them. The droplets gather around the protein particles and freeze to make snowflakes. Let the skiing continue!

Next year, try making a snow penguin!

Super snowball

US college students rolled the world's biggest snowball in 2013. It measured 10.04 m (32.94 ft) round and was 3.28 m (9.28 ft) high.

Scary snow

Snow looks beautiful, but it can be very dangerous. Here are some examples of times when snow can get scary.

A **blizzard** occurs when **heavy snowfall** combines with strong winds. In these conditions it's very hard to see. Cars can get stuck and people can get lost. The wind may blow the snow into drifts that might even become high enough to bury buildings.

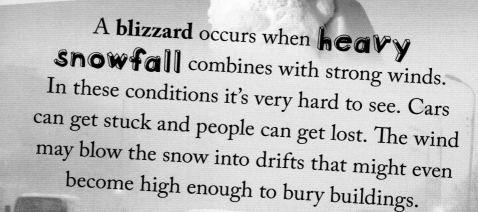

Falling snow makes driving dangerous

When snow blizzards are very thick, there can be **whiteouts**, when it becomes impossible to see anything through the snowflakes. In polar regions, a whiteout is something slightly different. It doesn't have to be snowing, but it does have to be cloudy over an unbroken blanket of snow. Then, if the sun reflects equally off the clouds and snow, everything appears to go white and it becomes impossible to tell the sky from the land.

An **avalanche** looks like a waterfall of snow thundering down a mountainside. It's caused when different layers of snow gradually build up on top of each other. If the layers are unstable, they may eventually slip over the top of each other, triggered by heavy winds, sudden rises in temperatures or vibrations.

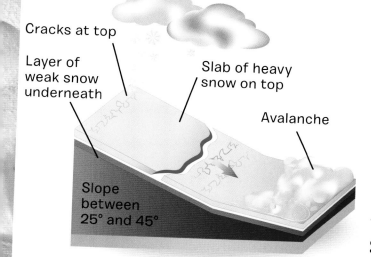

Cracks at top

Layer of weak snow underneath

Slab of heavy snow on top

Avalanche

Slope between 25° and 45°

Avalanche **safety**

In mountain areas prone to avalanches experts dig down to examine snow layers, looking for a layer that is full of air or made from ice pellets rather than snowflakes. These are the types of layers that can cause slippage. If the avalanche patrol thinks there is a threat, they will clear the area and trigger an avalanche using explosives to get rid of the unstable area of snow.

Record **fall**

Mount Baker in the USA holds the world record for the largest amount of snowfall in one ski season. Between 1998 and 1999 it had 2,896 cm (95 ft) of snow.

I like snow. It makes for a perfect penguin playground!

Small and stinging

In stormy weather you might find yourself pelted by tiny icy pellets called **hailstones**. Each one might be as small as a pea or (if you are unlucky!) as big as a golf ball.

Here comes the hail

Hailstones are made when raindrops are tossed up and down by strong winds inside a storm cloud. As a raindrop gets pushed high in the cloud it freezes. Then it falls and goes back up again, growing a new layer of ice each time it rises. Eventually the icy lump will be heavy enough to fall out of the cloud.

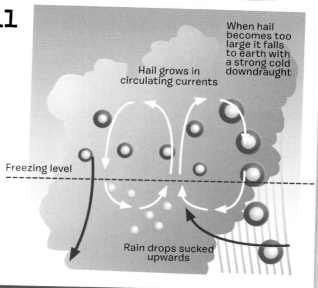

When hail becomes too large it falls to earth with a strong cold downdraught

Hail grows in circulating currents

Freezing level

Rain drops sucked upwards

The size of a hailstone will depend on what is happening inside the storm cloud. One of the biggest ever hailstones fell in Bangladesh in 1986. It was a monster, weighing 1 kg (2.2 lb). Big hailstones can smash windows and destroy crops, but the Bangladesh hailstorm was more serious, tragically killing 92 people.

Hail Alley is the nickname given to a belt of land east of the Rocky Mountains in the USA. It regularly gets severe thunderstorms and lots of hail. Farmers often see their crops battered by the ice pellets, and it's estimated they do around a billion US dollars worth of damage to crops and buildings every year.

An icy onion

If you cut a hailstone in half and looked at it under a microscope you would see lots of ice layers, rather like the inside of an onion.

Cloud-seeding planes (see p39) are sometimes used to try to shrink the hail in storm clouds, to make it less dangerous when it falls. The planes spray silver iodide pellets into the clouds so that lots of small hailstones will form round the pellets and fall harmlessly. In the past people rang church bells because they thought the sound might get rid of the hail clouds, but it wouldn't have had any effect.

I'd choose soft snowflakes any time.

Dewdrops and frosty fingers

In autumn, you might start to see spiders' webs hanging with tiny dewdrops. When low wintery temperatures come, the dew will be replaced by frost.

At night, the ground gets colder and so does the air above it. When conditions are cool enough, water vapour condenses out of the air just above the ground. You'll see it settled as **dew** on surfaces such as plants and cobwebs, in the evening and early morning in spring and autumn.

When the temperature is below freezing, water vapour condenses from the air above the ground, just as it does when dew is made. But this time it turns straight to ice crystals called **frost**. The tiny six-sided crystals gather together loosely and reflect light, which makes them look white.

You might see **frost** spreading out over a windowpane. It forms when very cold air is on the outside of a window and warmer moister air is on the inside. The window gets cold and water vapour condenses out of the warm air to make ice crystals. They gather in long branch-shapes on the glass.

Trees wrapped up to protect them from frost damage

Frost can badly damage some plants. Fruit farmers must be well prepared for frost if they don't want to lose their crop. For instance, in New Zealand's wine-growing country, helicopters sometimes fly over the grape vines at night to stir up the air above them and prevent frost.

Frosty face

In weather legends of northern Europe, Jack Frost brings the winter frosts. He is made of frost himself, with spiky-looking hair and fingers.

Jack Frost sounds cold-hearted!

Ice world

When the temperature is very cold water freezes, creating ice.

When the temperature dips in the winter time, dripping water freezes into long **icicles**. An icicle doesn't freeze all at once, but grows slowly downwards as the water drips. Some have been measured at over 8 m (26 ft) long!

An **ice storm**, also called a glaze storm, occurs when super-cold rain freezes on surfaces, coating everything in a thick ice layer. The heavy ice can even bring down trees and power lines. In the USA and Canada, where ice storms occur regularly, they can cause more damage than a hurricane and cost billions of dollars.

An **icebow**

An **icebow** is a freezing version of a rainbow. This time the sun shines through ice crystals in the air, instead of raindrops, and the bow-shape appears bright white.

Some **caves** are so cold they are permanently encrusted with ice. The world's biggest example is the Eisriesenwelt (the 'Ice Giant's World') a vast ice cave underneath the Alps in Austria. Melting snow drains into the cave from the mountains, and freezing cold winds blow through the cave and keep it frozen.

Polar bears fish in the freezing Arctic

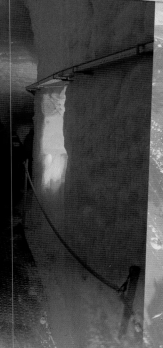

In the Arctic, the sea is always frozen at the North Pole. In the Antarctic, the land is always frozen at the South Pole. As well as this permanent ice, there are vast regions of polar ice that melt in summer and refreeze in winter. Find out how this could be changing on p78.

Penguins live on the Antarctic ice

I once fell asleep and an icicle grew off my beak.

Sharp look!

Ready to rumble

Are you ready for a rumble of thunder and a flash of lightning? This weather book is turning wild!

Hear the **skies roar**

A thunderstorm builds up when a pocket of warm, moist air shoots up into the sky, and keeps going until it gets to the top of the troposphere - which is when the anvil forms. The warm air creates a towering cumulonimbus cloud (see p37). Inside the cloud, violent winds toss around raindrops and hail, and electrical energy builds up. If there is enough energy in the cloud then thunder and lightning can occur.

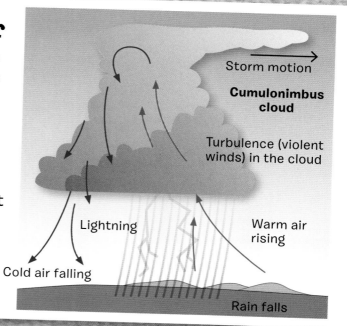

Storm motion

Cumulonimbus cloud

Turbulence (violent winds) in the cloud

Lightning

Warm air rising

Cold air falling

Rain falls

Thunder is the sound of air expanding very fast when it is heated up by super-hot lightning. Lightning and thunder happen at the same time but light travels faster than sound, so we see the lightning before we hear the sound it creates. The closer the lightning is to you, the louder the sound will be.

How far?

You can work out roughly how far away a storm is by counting the seconds between seeing a flash of lightning and hearing a clap of thunder. For every 3 seconds you count, the storm is 1 km (0.6 miles) away.

Thunderstorms are most likely to form in locations where the weather is hot and the air is moist, so tropical regions near sea coasts are a common thunderstorm spot. Meteorologists try to predict storms by studying weather radar and satellite images (see p87). In some countries, especially in America, trained **storm spotters** watch for signs of storms and give out warnings.

Storm spotters in a vehicle full of scientific equipment

Thunderstorm 3 top facts

1 The US National Weather Service estimates that there could be up to 40,000 thunderstorms on the planet every day. That's 14.6 million a year!

2 Most thunderstorms last around 30 minutes.

3 The biggest storm clouds are called supercell storm clouds. They stretch very high and can be up to 24 km (15 miles) wide.

The anvil top of a thundercloud seen from the Space Station

Was that thunder or your tummy rumbling?

Paths of light

Lightning is beautiful but super-dangerous. It can fork down to the ground or light up the whole sky.

Lightning occurs when electrical energy builds inside a storm cloud. Eventually it flashes out of the cloud as a super-fast and super-powerful spark. It travels down to the ground and back up again so fast it looks like one flash. A bolt can shoot down at speeds reaching 1,500 kph (932 mph) and shoot back up even faster. In its path the temperature is momentarily incredibly hot, up to five times hotter than the Sun.

Types of lightning

Lightning that hits the ground is called forked lightning. Lightning that flashes between clouds is called sheet lightning. Sheet lightning often looks as if it lights up the whole sky.

Lightning is very dangerous, and if it hits people it is likely to kill them instantly. It can cause instant fires where it strikes, too. A lightning bolt always takes the **quickest path** to the ground, so it tends to hit tall buildings and trees. Tall buildings must be fitted with a metal rod called a **lightning conductor**, which conducts the electricity safely to the ground if lightning strikes.

In 1752, American inventor Benjamin Franklin did a very dangerous experiment to discover that lightning was caused by electricity. He flew a kite in a thunderstorm with an iron key attached to the string, and a wire attached to the key was fixed on to a Leyden jar, which can store an **electrical charge**. This experiment was all to see if the electrical charge would flow down the wires into the jar but he was extremely lucky not to have been killed!

Lightning is awesome and scary at the same time!

A rare **mystery**

Ball lightning is a very rare and mysterious kind of lightning which looks like a glowing ball in the sky. It's possible that it occurs when lightning hits the ground and interacts with dust, but nobody knows for sure.

Superstorms

Hurricanes are huge swirling storms that form over the ocean. If they reach land they can cause a lot of damage.

On a satellite photo a hurricane looks like a giant whirling cloud with a hole in the centre which is called the eye of the hurricane. The eye could stretch up to 50 km (32 miles) wide. Here, in the middle of the roaring winds, the weather stays calm.

A tropical storm approaches

Weather experts try to predict how hurricanes will behave by studying satellite photos and taking measurements such as sea temperature and air pressure. The US Hurricane Hunter squadron goes even further, flying their planes into hurricanes to gather data.

Hurricane names

Hurricanes are also called typhoons and cyclones. They are given human names. The first hurricane of the season has a name beginning with A. The next one has a name beginning with B, and so on through the season.

Hurricanes form over the ocean in the **Tropics** (the regions around the Equator), where warm air full of water vapour rises over a large area. When the warm air rises as high as it can it flows outwards, cools and sinks, only to get sucked back into the storm. Clouds and strong winds begin to spread out and spin around the centre of the hurricane.

Hurricane Lewis in 1995, seen from space

Hurricane Gordon hit Miami, Florida in 1994

Hurricanes can take days to build up or just a few hours. They usually last two or three days before gradually dying out and once they make landfall (see p66) they quickly lose their power, since they rely on moisture from the warm sea surface for energy and to keep them going. At their height, hurricane windspeeds can reach 275 kph (160 mph) or more and the clouds can drop up to 9 trillion litres (2.4 trillion gallons) of rain in one day.

Wild weather days

If a hurricane arrives on land it can create a serious disaster, smashing up whole neigbourhoods and bringing flooding with it.

Hurricane Sandy approaches New York in 2012

The point where a hurricane arrives on land is called its '**landfall**'. It can bring with it a storm surge in the tide and big waves whipped up by the wind. Weather experts try to predict which way a hurricane will go and evacuate people if it's necessary.

Out at sea a hurricane can whip up huge **waves**. In 2004 Hurricane Ivan brought record-breaking 30.5 m (100 ft) waves to the Gulf of Mexico, the tallest waves ever measured at the time.

Waves lash northern Portugal

A hurricane force **wind** can come from any direction and change quickly. It may be strong enough to tear the roofs from buildings and carry dangerous debris in the air. People who live in hurricane regions must take steps such as putting hurricane shutters made of metal on their windows to try to stop damage to their homes.

Damage from Hurricane Sandy in 2012

Is it safe?
Areas less than 2,400 km (1,500 miles) from the Equator are most at risk from hurricanes, which usually occur from late spring to autumn.

The National Hurricane Center in Miami, Florida

Around 70% of the time, weather experts can accurately predict hurricanes a day in advance. Using data and specially designed computer programs they can predict a hurricane's size and how it will move. The predictions aren't always right though. For instance, in 1998 Hurricane Mitch was predicted to go west but it turned south into Central America, causing much destruction and flooding.

Always hide from a hurricane!

Evacuating New York from Hurricane Irene in 2011

67

Whirling winds

Thunderstorms and hurricanes prove that when warm air rises the weather can get wild. If the air then starts spinning, it can turn into a roaring funnel, smashing up everything in its path. Welcome to the awesome whirly world of tornadoes.

When warm air rises quickly and cools, thunderclouds develop (see p60). **Tornadoes** (also called **twisters**) are born underneath thunderclouds, when certain weather conditions are in place and the winds inside the cloud are going at different speeds and directions - the differences in pressure make the air start to spin, and the result is a giant whirling air funnel. If it reaches the ground it can smash up anything in its path, sucking up dust and debris like a giant vacuum cleaner.

Tornadoes vary in size and power. The biggest ones can spread over 3 km (2 miles) wide, and in the most powerful examples wind speeds can reach an incredible 500 kph (300 mph), powerful enough to smash up buildings. The twisters zoom across the ground at an average speed of around 50 kph (30 mph) for up to 15 minutes.

If a tornado forms over the sea or a lake it sucks up water, creating a giant **waterspout**. Waterspouts have been known to suck up lots of frogs or fish along with water, causing a weird rain of dead creatures to fall from the sky once the wind dies down.

Mammatus clouds at sunset

A mid-western stretch of the USA, nicknamed **Tornado Alley**, gets the most tornadoes in the world. Tornado-watchers try to predict they're coming by watching the clouds, especially keeping an eye on mammatus thunderclouds, which have an underside that looks like lots of rounded lumps.

People who have heard tornadoes say they sound like roaring jet planes or thundering waterfalls.

Tornado **types**

The Fujita Scale is used to measure tornado strength. Here are some of the key classifications.

F0
Minor damage to trees and buildings.

F1
Vehicles blown sideways off roads.

F2
Roofs torn off frame houses and large trees uprooted.

F3
Vehicles lifted off the ground and wooden buildings damaged.

F4
Vehicles picked up and carried over 2 km (1.2 miles).

F5
Total devastation in the path of the tornado.

Shimmer and shine

When the Sun blazes down, some unusual weather magic can happen!

A **mirage** looks like a pool of water up ahead on the ground on a blazing hot day (right). The water seems to ripple invitingly, but when you get close it's nowhere to be seen. It's really an **optical illusion**, a reflection of the sky onto a layer of hot air just above the ground. The hot air refracts (bends) the sunlight, creating the reflection effect.

Danger! Don't look!
Never look directly at the Sun. It could cause *permanent damage* to your eyes.

Sundogs are two bright spots that can appear either side of the Sun as part of an icebow. They're best seen when the Sun is low in the sky, and they are caused when sunlight is refracted as it passes through tiny ice crystals in high clouds.

Sundogs over the frozen Arctic Ocean

This page has lit up my life!

70

A sun pillar at sunrise in Voyageurs National Park, Minnesota, USA

A **sun pillar** is a shaft of light that seems to shine out from the sun at sunrise or sunset. It is created by the light shining onto millions of tiny ice crystals in clouds high above. It may change colour before gradually fading.

A sun pillar at sunrise in Voyageurs National Park, Minnesota, USA

Auroras are spectacular displays of dancing light in the sky, usually seen in the far north or south of the world. These aren't part of Earth's weather. They are actually caused when magnetically charged particles from the Sun enter the Earth's atmosphere and collide with gas particles there.

Auroras appear near the northern and southern magnetic poles. You need the right weather to see them

Dry times

When rainfall is unusually low, rivers and lakes dry up, and so does the soil. These extreme weather conditions are called **drought**.

Drought and hot weather can create the conditions for dangerous **bush fires**. Plants and trees become so dry that they easily burn and the hot weather can also bring gusty winds because the land heats up the air above it, making it rise (see p15). Wind makes bush fires much fiercer by fanning the flames.

When soil dries up it turns dusty. In some countries this leads to dusty **mini tornadoes** called **dust devils** (in Australia they are called willy-willies). These are created when a pocket of air heats up above the land and begins to spiral around, carrying dust and sand with it. Dust devils look spectacular racing across the landscape.

When strong winds pick up sand in desert regions, the result can be a raging **sandstorm** that stretches for many miles and engulfs everything in its path. This usually occurs in summer when the hot air over the land creates winds.

A sandstorm in Jordan

Some plants are drought-resistant, meaning they are adapted to survive in very dry weather. For instance, in Australia the Queensland bottle tree has its own water store in its trunk. In times of drought the Aboriginal people bore into the trunk to get water.

Spirit of the wind

Both Navajo Native Americans and Australian Aboriginal people believe that dust devils are the spirits of the dead. In Navajo legend, if the wind spins *clockwise* the dust devil is a good spirit. If it spins *anticlockwise*, the devil is a bad spirit.

Ouch! Sandstorms sting!

Power from the Sun

We can use the Sun's heat to create electricity and as long as the Sun shines, solar power will never run out!

Making Solar Power

We create **solar power** by using **photovoltaic cells**, called PCs for short. Sunlight is made up of tiny particles of solar energy called photons. When they hit a photovoltaic cell some of them are absorbed. The photons knock particles called electrons loose from the cell, which then flow around a circuit, making an electrical current.

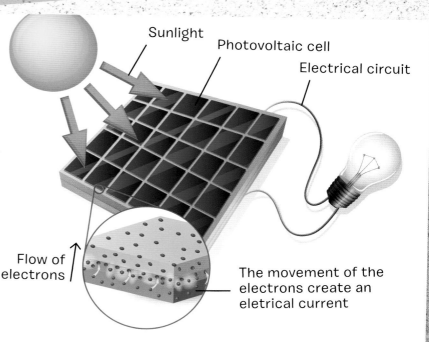

Sunlight

Photovoltaic cell

Electrical circuit

Flow of electrons

The movement of the electrons create an eletrical current

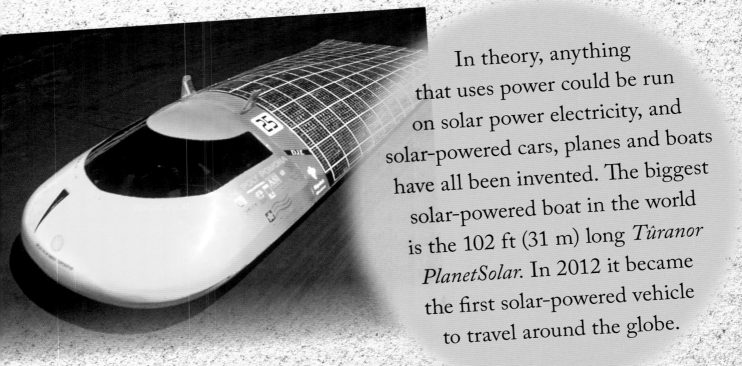

In theory, anything that uses power could be run on solar power electricity, and solar-powered cars, planes and boats have all been invented. The biggest solar-powered boat in the world is the 102 ft (31 m) long *Tûranor PlanetSolar*. In 2012 it became the first solar-powered vehicle to travel around the globe.

In regions where there is lots of sunshine, solar power is a great way to collect the energy needed to make **electricity**. At the Sahara Forest Project in Qatar (below) it is being used to grow plants too. Solar power is used to evaporate seawater, creating fresh water and cool air which gets circulated through greenhouses to grow cucumbers, tomatoes and peppers in the midst of a super-dry desert.

Solar-powered garden lights are a common sight

The giant Odeillo-Font-Romeu power station in the Pyrenees (below) is a **solar furnace**. Its system of mirrors reflects sunlight onto a central furnace, where extremely high temperatures are reached, hot enough to melt metal.

Solar power is hot!

Chapter 8: Tracking changes
Changes in history

Has the world's climate always been the same? Definitely not! There have been some pretty big changes in the history of our planet.

Dust thrown up by **mega-volcano** eruptions and meteor strikes has had a big effect on the weather in the past. Huge amounts of dust can block out the light of the Sun, killing plants and starving animals. It's thought that the dinosaurs might have died out this way, when a huge meteor hit the Earth.

A volcano erupts in Indonesia

Between 30,000 and 10,000 years ago the Earth's climate became very cold and much of the planet was covered in **ice sheets**. This frozen time is called the 'Last Great Ice Age'. Animals that were adapted to the cold, such as woolly mammoths, roamed the snowy icy wastes but died out around 10,000 years ago, when the climate began to warm up.

I wonder if there were ever woolly penguins?

When **glaciers** or ice sheets melt because of climate change, they leave clues behind. Glaciers carve U-shaped valleys as they move over the landscape and the rocks get picked up and pushed to the sides or the front of the **moving ice** river. When a glacier melts, piles of these rocks, called **moraines**, get left behind. We know from studying moraines around the planet that the last Ice Age ended around 10,000 years ago.

A U-shaped valley formed by a glacier

It's in the **trees**

It's possible to analyse climate by looking at tree rings. Trees grows a new ring every year, and the warmer and wetter the weather the thicker the ring grows.

We can find weather clues by studying accounts and images from history, and these have revealed that Europe and North America had a **mini Ice Age** between 1500 and 1850, when there were unusually cold temperatures. Rivers froze, winters were harsh and there were crop failures and famine.

Unusally, the River Thames in London, UK, froze in 1683

Changes now

We know that the Earth's climate can change over time, but it seems to be happening faster than ever.

At the top and bottom of the world there are giant permanent sheets of ice called **ice caps**. However, scientists monitoring them have found that they are beginning to get smaller. It's thought this may be due to an overall change in the world's air temperature, an effect that you will hear called **'climate change'**.

The Larsen B ice shelf in Antarctica. Space images have shown it beginning to break up.

The Perito Moreno Glacier in south Argentina

Many of the world's **glaciers** appear to be getting smaller. If they melted completely they would release so much water that sea levels would rise by several metres, flooding low-lying land. The cold water from the melting glaciers would lower sea temperatures.

If the sea temperature changes, the world's weather could change dramatically. Ocean currents carry warm or cool water around the planet. The water heats or cools the air above it, creating weather conditions such as regular rainfall. If the ocean currents alter, areas that once had regular rain might find they suffer drought, while others suffer from flooding.

No **snow**

Africa's highest mountain, Mount Kilimanjaro, was once covered in snow all year round. Now its permanent snows are disappearing and it could be snow-free by 2025.

When ice sheets break up there are more icebergs, which are dangerous to shipping

Severe drought in Australia

Many animals and plants could find themselves unable to survive due to **climate change**. For instance, polar bears rely on ice freezing in the far north every winter, so that they can search for seals to eat. In summer they wait on the shore for the ice to return, so they can feed once more. With the ice arriving later each year and lasting for less time, it is harder for the polar bears to find food and they are now endangered.

What about us penguins? Warming will affect our homes, too!

Ocean temperature changes may kill coral reefs

Could burning be to blame?

Could human activity be to blame for speeding up climate change and helping to change the world's weather?

The atmosphere is made up of nitrogen, oxygen, water vapour and smaller amounts of other gases, including CO_2 and methane. It absorbs the Sun's heat which warms up the planet surface. The heat then radiates back up into the air, keeping the temperature at an overall average of 15°C (59°F) which is just right for life to survive on Earth. If it changes, all life on Earth will be affected. This process is called **Global Warming**.

Could electricity use be speeding up climate change?

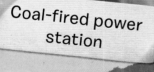
Coal-fired power station

In the last two centuries the world's population has grown quickly and industrialization has arrived. We now burn **fossil fuels** (coal, oil and natural gas) to create power, and this creates extra CO_2 which is released into the atmosphere. This is a '**greenhouse gas**', which means it absorbs heat radiated from the ground and reflects it back down, warming the atmosphere.

Methane is also a greenhouse gas, and we've been producing extra by creating giant rubbish landfills, which emit methane as they rot. Farming cattle makes methane, too. In fact the world's cows produce so much methane by burping and farting that some scientists think they have a worse effect on the environment than cars.

Deforestation in Madagascar

Trees store a huge amount of the world's **carbon**. When they are cut down and burnt, either as fuel or to clear land, the carbon is released into the air as CO_2. The world's rainforests in particular are rapidly being cleared to make farmland - this is known as deforestation. It's thought that this could be contributing to global warming.

Saving resources

Many people are trying to help cut the emission of greenhouse gases by making changes in their daily lives. That means recycling waste and trying to burn less fossil fuel by cutting down on electricity use.

By **recycling** our waste we can help cut down the rotting methane-producing waste in landfill sites. We can help to lessen waste of the world's resources, too. Here's what happens to materials you recycle:

▶ Newspaper gets recycled to make new paper.
▶ Garden and kitchen waste gets recycled to make plant fertilizer.
▶ Glass can be made into new glass.
▶ Plastic can be made into new plastic goods such as bottles, seed trays and CD cases. You can even get fleece jackets made from recycled plastic bottles.

Many cities have bike rental schemes to reduce car use

Save power and help save the planet!

Earth Hour

Every year, on the last Saturday in March, millions of people all over the world switch off their building lights for an hour to raise awareness of global warming and to save power. It is called Earth Hour, and was begun by the Worldwide Fund for Nature.

Vehicles that burn petrol in their engines emit CO_2 particles from their exhausts. Hybrid cars, which run partly on electricity, emit less CO_2. Electric cars, which run on electricity alone, emit no CO_2. However, the electricity they use is made at power stations which give out CO_2, so electric cars are not pollution-free. Engineers are working hard to design car engines that make less pollution.

Electric cars plugged in to recharge

An eco-friendly house

Modern homes are built with eco-friendly features so that they use less energy and water. Good wall insulation (padding) can conserve heat inside the house while solar panels and a wind turbine can provide power. An eco-friendly home would also have appliances that use less water and power. Even if you live in an older home, you can make sure it is insulated properly and try not to over-use electricity and water.

Greenhouse gases

These approximate figures from the US government show the breakdown of human activities that give out greenhouse gases.

3% Methane and other greenhouse gases emitted from landfill waste.

8% Commercial and residential buildings.

13% Transport using petrol-based fuels.

14% Agriculture, particularly livestock, rice production and peat-burning.

26% The burning of coal, natural gas and oil to make electricity and heat.

19% Fossil fuels burnt and chemicals emitted at industrial sites such as factories.

17% Deforestation. The burning of forests to create farmland.

See – no fossil fuel!

As well as solar power, other energy sources are used to try to cut down on the emission of greenhouse gases.

The heat from hot underground springs can be harnessed to provide **geothermal energy**. In Iceland, where there are lots of hot springs, over 25% of the country's electricity is created this way, and the energy is also used directly to heat homes and provide hot water.

A geothermal power plant at the Blue Lagoon in Iceland

Ocean currents and tides are always moving, and the movement can be used to turn underwater turbines that generate electricity. The turbines are positioned to move in the direction of the tides each day.

The Rance Tidal Power Station in France has generated power since 1966

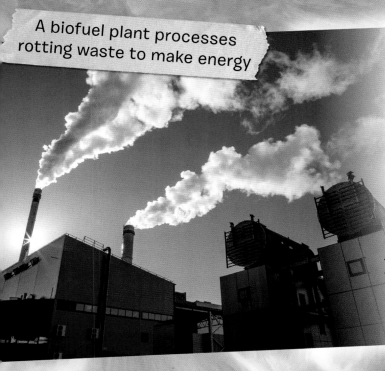
A biofuel plant processes rotting waste to make energy

Bioreactor plants can help to create power from **waste**. In a bioreactor on a landfill site, the waste is treated to make it rot more quickly. Then the methane gas produced by the rotting waste is burnt to create electricity. This prevents methane from reaching the atmosphere, and fossil fuels are not used in the power-making process.

The race is on to develop everyday fuels that don't emit greenhouse gases, either in the process of being made or being used. One option is hydrogen, which can be combined with oxygen in a **fuel cell** to make electricity, heat and water without any pollution. Space vehicles are powered by hydrogen fuel cells, and the astronauts on board get the added bonus of clean water to drink.

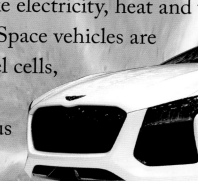

Many car makers are developing fuel cells for cars

The **champions**

Norway is the world's greenest fuel country. It supplies all of its energy needs using renewable power and has some left over to sell to other countries.

The Vermork hydroelectric plant in Norway

Here's hoping my ice doesn't melt!

Chapter 9: Working with the weather
Evidence hunting

Meteorologists gather all the information they can in order to try to predict the weather.

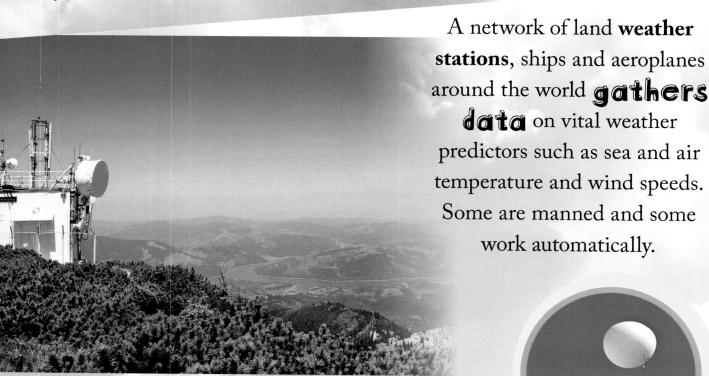

A network of land **weather stations**, ships and aeroplanes around the world **gathers data** on vital weather predictors such as sea and air temperature and wind speeds. Some are manned and some work automatically.

Weather **buoys** bob up and down on the ocean, measuring information such as air pressure and humidity. Meanwhile unmanned **weather balloons** fly up to 40 km (25 miles) high or more, carrying weather-measurement equipment. The data from the balloons can be transmitted back to Earth via satellite.

Weather **satellites** orbit the Earth carrying data-measuring equipment. They have cameras for taking ordinary images as well as infrared images which show heat-emission from down below. The images can be used to study the shape of clouds and spot if storms are forming.

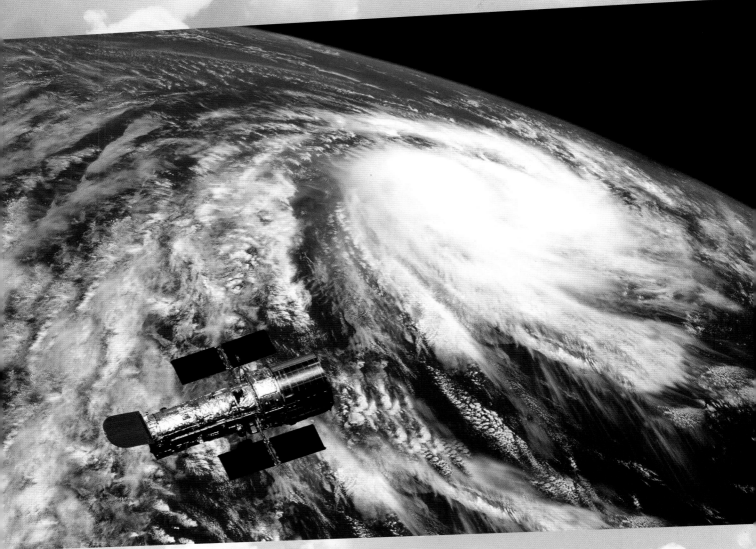

Satellite **radar** equipment is used to measure rainfall around the planet. Radar waves are fired down into the atmosphere and they bounce back off raindrops. Antennae sense their return and the data is transmitted to Earth, where it is converted into computer images that show the location and intensity of the rain. Thunderstorms and hurricanes can be spotted by radar, too.

Weather lore

For centuries people have tried to predict the weather in weird and wonderful ways. How successful were they?

Keep an eye on **pinecones** to forecast the **humidity**. The cones tend to open their scales in dry air and close up in humid air. Air tends to become more humid before wet weather.

Long before barometers were invented, native tribes in northeastern North America had their own weather-predictor – a **weather stick** – and it's still sometimes used in the USA. The stick, from a balsam fir tree, is mounted outside pointing sideways. It bends down when rain is coming and bends up when the weather is fair. The stick bends because its tiny cells contract or expand, depending on moisture in the air.

I can predict the weather where I live. It's going to be cold!

Some **animals** behave differently when they sense changes in air pressure. Scientists monitoring shark behaviour found they swam to deeper safer waters when hurricanes approached, probably because they sensed a pressure drop. Migrating birds decide when to begin their journeys depending on the air pressure, as its best for them to fly in fine weather.

All **sit**

One famous weather saying is that cows sit down when it's going to rain. In fact, this is what cow-studying scientists have discovered:

▶ Cows stand up more in hot weather, to reduce their body temperature.
▶ Cows sit down more in cold weather, to conserve their body heat.
▶ Cold weather often brings rain (though not always).

On February 2nd every year a **groundhog** called Phil predicts the weather at a grand ceremony in Punxsutawney, Pennsylvania, USA. Legend has it that if he comes out of his temporary den and sees his shadow he will go back in, signalling that winter will go on for six more weeks.

And now the weather
in the rest of the Solar System

What weather would space travellers have to cope with if they went to other planets? We know from data sent back by space probes that the weather is pretty wild up there!

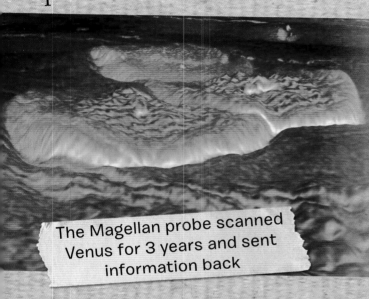

The Magellan probe scanned Venus for 3 years and sent information back

Venus is the hottest planet in the Solar System because it's surrounded by dense clouds of CO_2. They cause a serious greenhouse effect, keeping the planet surface very hot. Super-strong winds whip through the poisonous clouds. On the surface, the air pressure is a crushing 90 times the air pressure at sea level on Earth.

Jupiter has huge storms that last for centuries and cover wide areas. Its famous **Great Red Spot** is actually a permanent raging storm over 40,000 km (24,855 miles) wide. The planet is covered with thick poisonous cloud, has super-powerful lightning and winds whipping along at up to 360 kph (220 mph).

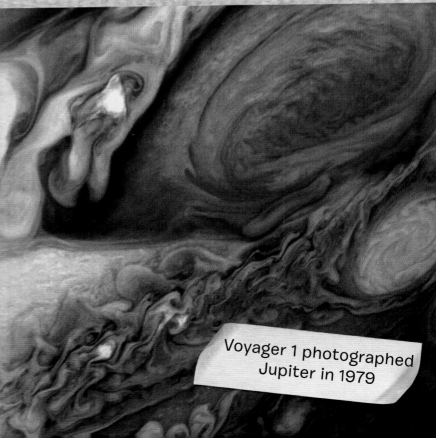

Voyager 1 photographed Jupiter in 1979

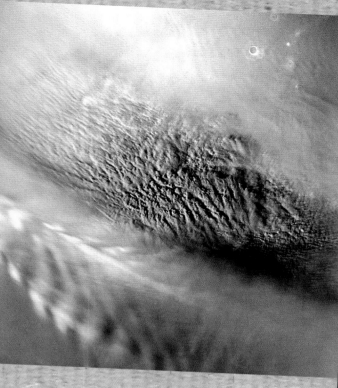

The **Martian** weather varies, but we know the planet never has rain because its atmosphere is too cold. Sometimes it is so chilly that CO_2 in the atmosphere turns to dry ice and falls to the surface. Occasionally the wind whips up, creating giant dust storms that last for weeks.

The Hubble Space Telescope saw a dust storm that covered Mars for two months in 2001

Today in space
You can go online and find out the exact weather on Mars today, as measured by NASA's space satellites and probes.

Let's not plan a picnic in space any time soon!

Fierce forecasts
How about our other Solar System neighbours? Here are their weather forecasts, and they don't sound good!
- Mercury – either super-hot or frigidly cold.
- Saturn – massive storms that go on for months, with huge lightning bolts.
- Neptune – really wild weather, with incredibly strong winds of up to 2,100 kph (1,305 mph).
- Uranus – unbelievably cold poisonous clouds whirling around.

Glossary

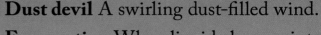

Acid rain Rain that contains damaging acidic chemicals.

Air mass A large body of air that has equal temperature, air pressure and humidity (amount of water vapour).

Air pressure The weight of air molecules in the atmosphere.

Anemometer An instrument for measuring wind strength.

Atmosphere The gases that surround our planet.

Barometer An instrument for measuring air pressure.

Beaufort Scale A number system for measuring wind speed. It ranges from 0 (calm) to 12 (hurricane).

Blizzard Heavy snowfall combined with strong wind.

Climate Weather conditions in a location over many years.

Cloud-seeding Firing particles into clouds to make raindrops form.

Condensation/Condenses When gas changes into a liquid.

Dew point The temperature at which water vapour condenses out of the air.

Doldrums Regions near the Equator where air pressure is low.

Dust devil A swirling dust-filled wind.

Evaporation When liquid changes into gas.

Flash flooding Sudden flooding caused by a heavy downpour.

Front The front edge of an air mass where it meets an air mass of a different temperature.

Glacier A slow-moving river of ice.

Greenhouse gases Gases in the Earth's atmosphere that reflect back the heat that radiates from the Earth's surface.

Humidity The amount of water vapour in the air.

Hurricane A severe tropical cyclone with winds over 116 kph (73 mph).

Icebow A freezing version of a rainbow, when the Sun shines through ice crystals in the air. Also know as a halo.

Ice storm When rain freezes on surfaces, coating everything in a thick ice layer.

Isobar A line drawn on a weather map connecting locations which have the same air pressure (measured to sea level) at a given time.

Jet stream A regular flow of very strong wind high up in the atmosphere.

Lightning conductor A metal rod fitted to a tall structure, to conduct electricity safely to the ground when lightning strikes.

Meteorologist Someone who studies the weather.

Microclimate A climate that is specific to a local area, such as a city, and is different from the area around it.

Millibar A measurement of air pressure.

Mirage An optical illusion of water on the ground, caused by sunlight.

Monsoon Seasonal changes in wind direction that bring rains to southern Asia, western Africa and northern Australia.

Moraine A pile of rock left behind by a glacier.

Photovoltaic cell Equipment for converting the Sun's energy into electricity.

Prevailing wind A wind that generally blows one way at a particular location or season

Refraction/Refracted Bending of light.

Smog A mixture of smoke and fog.

Solar power Energy created by the sun and transformed into electricity.

Tornado A whirling column of air around a centre with very low pressure.

Tropics The regions around the Equator.

Troposphere The atmosphere from sea level to around 14 km (8.6 miles) high. Weather occurs here.

Trade winds Winds that regularly blow on either side of the Equator.

Weathering Wearing down of the landscape by the weather.

Weather balloon A large gas-filled balloon that carries weather-measuring instruments into the air.

Weather station A collection of weather-measuring instruments for gathering data such as rainfall and air temperature.

Index

Picture credits

Every effort has been made to trace the copyright holders, and we apologise in advance for any unintentional omissions. We would be pleased to insert the appropriate acknowledgement in any subsequent edition of this publication.

Alamy blickwinkel 50 bl; Mike Abrahams 18 bl

Getty Images Brandenburg 39 ar; Alexander Joe 47 br; Antar Dayal 4 al; DEA/G Cargagna 9 ar; Ed Darack 64 cl; Friedrich Bouterwek 8 bl; Heritage Images 77 bl; Hulton Archive 63 cr; Joe Raedle 67 cl; Mark Wilson 61 ar; Michael & Patricia Fogden 46 bl; Mondadori Portfolio 6 bl; Nigel Pavitt 43 bga; Ralph Wetmore 62 bg; Scott B Smith Photography 65 bl; Thomas Northcut 11 bl; WIS Bernard 49 ar

NASA E De Jong et al 90 al; NASA 4 bg, 61 b, 65 bg, 78 ar; NASA/JPL 90 al; NASA/JPL-Caltech/MSSS 91 al; NASA/JPL/USGS 91cr

Courtesy of **Rustic Log Creations** 88 b, cl & l

Shutterstock 7382489561 84ar; Ahmad A Atwah 73ar; Alan Freed 89bl; AlenKadr 20 bg; Alexander Chelmodeev 33 cr; Alexey Stiop 69 br; American Spirit 74 bl; Amor Kar 94 a; Andrzej Kubik 72 br; any_keen 69 bcr; aodaodaodaod 31 br; Araleboy 72 bg; ArTDi101 57 ar; Asianet-Pakistan 4 ar; baitong333 80 l; Barry Blackburn 39 al; bibiphoto 48 br; BigRoloImages 79 ac; bikeriderlondon 59 br; BlueOrange Studio 21 br; BlueRingMedia 74 a; bogdan ionescu5 bl; Bos11 89 a; Bplanet 54 bg; Brandon Bourdages 7 al; Carlos Caetano 15 cr; Casther 28 bg; Cathy Kovarik 67 ar; Cher_Nika 50 bg; Christophe Testi 35 bl; Christopher Wood 13 ac; clearviewstock 86 cr; ClimberJAK 53 bc; CreativeNature.nl 83 cl; Daimond Shutter 16 cl; Dainis Derics 4 br, 50 cr, Dan Schreiber 45 cl; Daniel J. Rao 42 br; Daniel Prudek 13 al; De Visu 24 br; Dennis van de Water 81 bl; Dervin Witmer 69 bc; Designua 13 bc, 21 ar, 25 ar, 53 cl; dogi 82 c; Donald Bowers Photography 66 bga; EricIsselee 6 cr, 9 br, 11 br, 16 br, 18 bc, 23 bc, 36 b, 39 bc, 81 ar; erichon 40 al; Ethan Daniels 79 br; Eugene Sergeev 56 ar; FloridaStock 59 cl; fongfong 5 br; Foto by M 85 cr; Glamorous Images 35 al; GOLFX 42 bbg; hafakot 57 cl; Haris Vythoulkas 6 cl; Henk Bentlage 88 ar; Hung Chung Chih 49 bl; hraska 24 bg; Iain Frazer 75 br; Igumnova Irina 52 cr; Ingrid Curry 34 bl; Ivan Pavlov 59; Janelle Lugge 72 al; Jason Patrick Ross 60 bgb; javarman 30 br; jlelelr 37 bgb; John Huntington 22 bg; Julio Aldana 7 cr; jurgajurga 77 c; Juriaan Wossink 44 bg; kazoka 53 bg; kenny1 69 cl; KENNY TONG 7 bl, 94 b; kojihirano 23 cr; Konstantin Romanov 85 al; kosam 69 bcl; L Barnwell 69 bl;

Iafoto 69 bga; Lavinia Bordea 86 al; Leksele 6 c; 35 b; Leonid Ikan 19 bl; leungchopan 80 r; Lissandra Melo 22 br; Loskutnikov 70 ar; Marafona 5 al, 22 cl; MarArt 31 ar; MarcelClemens 54 bl, 93 br; Marco Regali 13 cl; Marina Vlasova 34 cl; Mark Caunt 31 cl; Mark Payne 52 bl, 96 b; Mary Terriberry 41 cr; Matt Gibson 46 bg; meunierd 28 cr, 78 bl; Michael Thaler 89 cr; Mikael Damkier 19 al; Mikko Lemola 58 b; Mimadeo 34 br; MIMOHE 86 b; mumbojumbo 73 c; natalia bulatova 55 bl; Nemar74 41 al; Nicku 64 ar; Olaf Speier 57 bc; onime 5 ar, 76 al; Orhan Cam 29 cl; patjo 77 ar; patpitchaya 38 bg; pchais 10 b; pedrosala 29 a; Pefkos 27 bgb; Pete Spiro 58 cl; PeterPhoto123 34 ar; Picsfive 46 cl; Pi-Lens 76 br; Pukhov Konstantin 58 ar; pzAxe 9 bl; R Kristoffersen 4 bl; R. Gino Santa Maria 68 bl; Radoslaw Lecyk 47 bga; Robert Adrian Hillman 18 ar; Rodionov Oleg 75 cl; S_E 63 a; Sanchai Kumar 16 ar; Santi Rodriguez 14 ar; Scandphoto 85 bl; Sean Pavone 67 br; siro46 10 bg; Silberkorn 51 ar; Solodov Alexey 23 ar; Sopotnicki 83 ar; Sorin Vidis 35 ar; sunsinger 11 cb, 15 bbg; SurangaSL 71 b; Surne1shots 55 ar; swa182 37 bga, 45 ar, 68 bgc; T photography 43 br; Toth Tamas 56 bl; TTphoto 36 bga; Tudor Spinu 22 bl; ucchie79 24 al; Ungnoi Lookjeab 48 al; urosr 40 br; Vladimir Melnikov 35 br; Vova Shevchuk 51 cr; Warren Goldswain 14 bl; Watchtheworld 22 bcl; Yen Hung 32 bgc; Zacarias Pereira da Mata 66 br

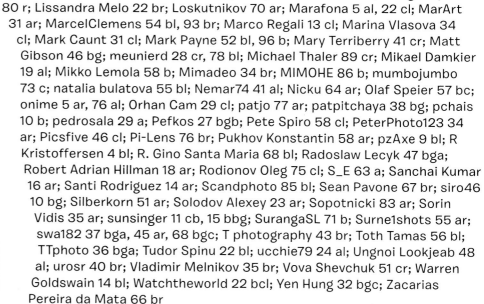

Thinkstock Image House/acollectionRF 30 bg; karinegenest 70 b; RobertHoetink 22 bcr; catolla 1 main; 30 cl; Gargolas 82 cl; iSailorr 40 bg; JohnCarnemolla 79 cl; milangonda 37 br; narongcp 44 bga; RolfAasa 12 br; rypson 37 ac; trekandshoot 49 bg; wissanu_phiphithaphong 36 bgb